Martin Luther KING JR.

DAVID DOWNING

Heinemann
LIBRARY

www.heinemann.co.uk/library
Visit our website to find out more information about Heinemann Library books.

To order:
☎ Phone 44 (0) 1865 888066
▤ Send a fax to 44 (0) 1865 314091
▨ Visit the Heinemann Bookshop at www.heinemann.co.uk/library to browse our catalogue and order online.

First published in Great Britain by Heinemann Library,
Halley Court, Jordan Hill, Oxford OX2 8EJ,
a division of Reed Educational and Professional Publishing Ltd.
Heinemann is a registered trademark of Reed Educational and Professional Publishing Ltd.

OXFORD MELBOURNE AUCKLAND
JOHANNESBURG BLANTYRE GABORONE
IBADAN PORTSMOUTH (NH) USA CHICAGO

Designed by AMR
Illustrated by Art Construction
Originated by Dot Gradations
Printed in China

ISBN 0 431 13867 2 (hardback)   ISBN 0 431 13874 5 (paperback)
06 05 04 03   07 06 05 04 03
10 9 8 7 6 5 4 3 2   10 9 8 7 6 5 4 3 2 1

British Library Cataloguing in Publication Data
Downing, David
  Martin Luther King Jr. – (Leading lives)
  1.King, Martin Luther, 1929–1968 2.African American civil
  rights workers – Biography – Juvenile literature 3.United
  States – Politics and government – 20th century – Juvenile
  literature 4.United States – History – 20th century
  Juvenile literature
  1.Title
  323.1'196'073'092

Acknowledgements
The publishers would like to thank the following for permission to reproduce photographs:
Associated Press: pp. 5, 13, 17, 19, 21, 24, 27, 33, 42, 43, 49, 51, 52, 53, 56; Camera press: pp. 7, 38; Corbis: pp. 6, 9, 14, 30; Popperfoto: pp. 34, 39, 45, 47; Sylvia Pitcher: p. 40; Time Magazine: p. 22.

Cover photograph reproduced with permission of Corbis.

Every effort has been made to contact copyright holders of any material reproduced in this book. Any omissions will be rectified in subsequent printings if notice is given to the publishers.

Our thanks to Christopher Gibb for his comments in the preparation of this book.

Disclaimer
All the Internet addresses (URLs) given in this book were valid at the time of going to press. However, due to the dynamic nature of the Internet, some addresses may have changed, or sites may have ceased to exist since publication. While the author and publishers regret any inconvenience this may cause readers, no responsibility for any such changes can be accepted by either the author or the publishers.

Any words appearing in the text in bold, **like this**, are explained in the Glossary.

Contents

1 Southern night

On the night of 30 January 1956, a bomb explodes in a quiet street of the small American city of Montgomery, Alabama. The veranda of a house is torn in two, its windows shattered and front rooms filled with broken glass. The owner of the house, the local **African American** preacher Martin Luther King Jr., is out addressing a political meeting, but his wife and baby daughter are at home.

Informed of the attack, the 27-year-old King rushes home in his car, his mind whirring with dreadful possibilities. He has been half expecting something like this; as leader of the current campaign to **integrate** the buses of Montgomery he knows there will be attempts to scare him off, even to kill him. He does not know the names of those responsible, but he knows what they are – white men who cannot face the idea of a society in which races mingle freely on an equal basis.

Outside his house he finds a large African American crowd confronting a few nervous-looking white policemen. Inside he finds that his wife Coretta and daughter Yolanda are upset but otherwise unharmed. As the white mayor and police chief tell King that they regret this 'unfortunate incident', they cast anxious glances through the shattered windows at the crowd outside. Perhaps they hear one man shout to a policeman: 'You've got your thirty-eight [gun], and I got mine – let's shoot it out.'

King goes outside, holds up a hand, and the crowd falls absolutely silent. 'My wife and baby are all right,' he says. 'I want you to go home and put down your weapons. We cannot solve this problem through retaliatory violence …

We must love our white brothers, no matter what they do to us … Jesus still cries out across the centuries, "Love your enemies." This is what we must live by. We must meet hate with love.'

Silently the crowd melts away into the night. One policeman tells a reporter: 'I owe my life to that nigger preacher, and so do all the other white people who were there.'

King will spend the next twelve years appealing to the good in people, breaking down barriers as he does so. After leading the **civil rights** campaign to victory in **the South** he will go on to question the way his country treats its poor and how it behaves abroad. By the time an assassin finally succeeds in killing him, 'that nigger preacher' will have become one of the greatest Americans of that and any other century.

◄ *Martin Luther King Jr. with officials on the bombed veranda of his house in Montgomery, Alabama.*

Childhood and youth

On 15 January 1929, a second child was born to Alberta and Martin Luther King in Atlanta, Georgia. The boy was named after his father, but known by his initials, M.L. A younger brother, Alfred Daniel (A.D.), soon joined M.L., his older sister Christine, parents and grandmother in the large two-storey house on Auburn Avenue, the main thoroughfare of that part of the city where **African Americans** (American descendants of African slaves) lived.

▲ The house on Auburn Avenue, Atlanta, where Martin Luther King Jr. was born in 1929.

Martin Luther King Sr. had risen from poor beginnings. His father, a **sharecropper** in rural Georgia, drank too much and beat his wife, and Martin Sr. escaped from home as soon as he could, striking out for Atlanta at the age of fifteen. He got work as a mechanic's assistant and a railroad fireman, and put himself through high school in his after-work hours. He started preaching, and in 1926 met and married Alberta, the daughter of Reverend Adam Williams, the **pastor** of the Ebenezer Baptist Church. When the Reverend Williams died in 1931, Martin Sr. took over as pastor.

◀ The church in Atlanta, Georgia where Martin's father was pastor from 1931 until 1975.

The boy

The Kings were a prosperous family. Martin Sr. proved both a popular **minister** and a clever businessman; Alberta, a quiet woman with a peaceful temperament, proved the perfect minister's wife. Martin Jr. not only grew up in a loving and comfortable family, he also enjoyed being part of the caring community of his father's church.

He was a clever boy, memorizing hymns and long passages from the Bible by the time he was five years old, but he also liked baseball, riding his bicycle, and playing with his kite and model planes. Martin Sr. occasionally punished his children's bad behaviour by beating them with a leather strap, but Martin Jr. always had great love and respect for his father. He was a sensitive child, who tended to take responsibility for the misfortunes of others. When his much-loved grandmother died, Martin Jr. was watching a parade in town. He felt so guilty for not being at her side he threw himself out of a second-floor window, bruising himself badly.

Martin Jr. could hardly have hoped for a better home to grow up in, but the world beyond was another matter entirely. The first hint of this came when he was about five: his white friends' mother told him her two boys were getting too old to play with a black child. His parents tried to explain why this had happened, taking him through the history of African Americans, from slavery to **segregation**. 'You must never feel you are less than anybody else,' his mother told him.

Jim Crow

There was no doubting the fact that African Americans were treated as inferiors by most white Americans. As he grew up, Martin Jr. found himself surrounded by ignorance and prejudice. Across the American **South**, whites and African Americans went to different schools, libraries, parks, restaurants, swimming pools and drinking fountains. The African American facilities were always inferior to the white facilities. At shops they had to use side windows, in cinemas they were restricted to the balcony. This system of segregation was kept in place by a huge number of state, city and county legal restrictions known as the 'Jim Crow' laws.

YOU CAN LOCATE THE AREA KNOWN AS 'THE SOUTH' ON THE MAP ON PAGE 29.

'The South'

When people talk about the 'the South', they usually mean those south-eastern states of the USA which refused to end slavery until forced to do so by defeat in the American Civil War (1861–65). These were Virginia, North Carolina, South Carolina, Georgia, Florida, Alabama, Mississippi, Tennessee, Louisiana, Arkansas and Texas. However, officially approved **racial discrimination** continued in these states, to differing degrees, for nearly 100 more years.

▲ A segregated drinking fountain in the American South. As a child, Martin became aware of the laws that enforced segregation like this.

Martin Jr.'s father, a prominent member of the Atlanta section of the NAACP (National Association for the Advancement of Colored People), refused to accept this was the way things should be. On one occasion he was out in the car with Martin Jr. when a white policeman stopped him and called him 'boy'. 'See that child there,' Martin Sr. responded, pointing at Martin Jr.: 'that is a boy. I am a man.' On another occasion, he walked out of a shoe shop with his elder son rather than use segregated black seats at the back. 'I don't care how long I have to live with the system,' he told Martin. 'I am never going to accept it. I'll fight it till I die'.

The young man

Atlanta was a big city with a fair-sized African American middle class, so Martin Jr. was able to attend one of the better African American schools in the South. He was a great success there, academically and socially. He particularly enjoyed English and history. By his early teens, he had developed an interest in opera, was playing the violin, and had begun to enjoy public speaking. His rich baritone voice, his fondness for dressing smartly and his skill on the dance floor soon made him popular with the girls. He was also very fond of his food, particularly traditional Southern dishes like fried chicken, cornbread and collard greens (kale).

In his last year of school he entered a state-wide debating competition. At the final, held in a small Georgian town, he won first prize for his presentation *The Negro and the Constitution*, but he was not allowed to enjoy his triumph for long. On the bus home to Atlanta, he and his teacher were forced to give up their seats for whites, and Martin stood for the rest of the long journey, almost shaking with anger at the injustice of it all.

A brief history of African Americans

The first African slaves were brought to the Americas in 1518. Over the next three centuries some fifteen million African men, women and children were landed in what is now known as the USA, but many more died during the Atlantic crossings. Slaves were worked to the limits of their strength, badly fed and housed. They had no legal rights. Families were often split up and women were abused by their white masters.

After the USA won independence from Great Britain in 1776, the trade in slaves was abolished but slavery continued in the South. Pressure from northern states eventually resulted in the defeat of the South in the American Civil War (1861–65). Slaves were then freed and African Americans were officially guaranteed equal rights.

However, in the defeated South, African Americans' rights were reduced until they were treated like slaves by many white people. The first major African American organization to fight against this was the NAACP, which said that discrimination should be fought in the law courts rather than on the streets. **Integration** of African Americans into white-dominated society was minimal right up to the landmark Montgomery bus **boycott** in 1955 (see pages 16–21).

3 College

In 1944, many of America's young men — black and white — were abroad fighting World War II and colleges filled the resulting spaces with gifted boys who would previously have been considered under-age. That spring, aged only 15, Martin Jr. took and passed the entrance exam to Atlanta's Morehouse College. He would begin his studies there in September.

That summer he took a job on a tobacco farm in the north-eastern state of Connecticut. It was hard work, but in the evenings he and his fellow Southerners enjoyed the freedoms of a **desegregated** society, eating wherever they chose and entering cinemas by the front door. On the train home to Georgia, Martin was reminded of the differences in **the South**: a curtain was pulled around his dining table so his presence would not upset white diners.

Morehouse

Morehouse was one of the most respected African American colleges in the South, and the discussion of racial matters was encouraged. Martin already knew he wanted to help his community, but was not sure how he should do so. He was not convinced he should follow his father into the church. His mind rebelled against the literal interpretation of the Bible favoured by most **African American** and white Southern churchmen; it seemed too simple and unsophisticated. He had also often found himself embarrassed by his father's highly emotional **sermons**. Perhaps medicine or the law would offer more scope for his intelligence.

The Morehouse principal, Dr Benjamin Mays, helped him decide, by asking, what other institution in the black community had such potential for leading the way towards social and political change?

▲ A lecture at Morehouse College. The opportunity to discuss racial issues at Morehouse gave Martin the start in his lifelong campaign to improve conditions for African Americans.

So, when he was seventeen years old, Martin successfully gave a trial sermon at his father's church. Later that year he was **ordained** and made assistant **pastor**.

Crozer

After graduating from Morehouse in 1948, he enrolled for a BA course in Divinity at Crozer Theological Seminary, a mixed-race religious college in Chester, Pennsylvania. For the next three years he studied the works of the great philosophers and religious thinkers.

He became an admirer of two men who had combined religious faith with rebellion against their governments: the white American Henry David Thoreau and the Indian Mohandas Gandhi. Thoreau served a jail sentence for refusing to pay taxes to a government that supported slavery, and in 1849 wrote an essay called *On the Duty of Civil Disobedience*, which later influenced Gandhi.

◀ *Mohandas Gandhi, whose philosophy of civil disobedience and the 'force of truth' had a strong influence on King.*

Gandhi launched several **civil disobedience** campaigns against British **colonialism** between 1919 and 1943, relying on *satyagraha* – the 'force of truth' – rather than violence to undermine his opponents.

This idea greatly excited the young Martin Luther King Jr. Why could American blacks not appeal to white American consciences with their own 'soul force', the power of Christian love?

Boston

After graduating at the top of his class in 1951, King signed on for a **doctorate** course at Boston University's School of Theology. He was a hard-working student, but also enjoyed Boston's social life, particularly its restaurants and jazz clubs. He went out with several young women, but he was beginning to get bored with the life of a bachelor when he met Coretta Scott. On their first date he told her she had character, intelligence, personality and beauty, the four things that he looked for in a wife.

Coretta, who came from a much poorer Southern family, was a student singer at the New England Conservatory of Music. She had no intention of giving up her career to become a preacher's wife, but the young King's blend of seriousness and enthusiasm for life won her round. On 18 June 1953, they were married by Martin Sr. in her family's garden in Marion, Alabama.

Back in Boston, King started applying for jobs as a pastor. In the spring of 1954 he gave a trial sermon at the Dexter Avenue Baptist Church in Montgomery, Alabama, and a few weeks later was offered the job.

He and Coretta talked through the pros and cons of returning to the South. That same spring the **Supreme Court** declared that segregated schools were illegal – it seemed as if things were beginning to change at last. Much as he loved his academic life and the greater freedoms of the North, King felt it was his duty to go back, and Coretta could not argue with him. In September 1954 they set up home in the heart of the old South.

A key decision

In May 1954, in the case of Brown v. Board of Education, the Supreme Court outlawed separate educational facilities, saying that they were bound to be unequal. Segregated schools, the Court said, created a feeling of inferiority' among African Americans that might 'affect their hearts and minds in a way unlikely to be undone'. But although such schools were now illegal, many states and cities, particularly in the South, continued to operate them in defiance of the law.

4 Montgomery and the bus boycott

The Kings' first year in Montgomery was busy but quiet. They lived in a house on a shady street, and Martin got used to his duties at the church, conducting marriages and funerals, advising on family problems, and delivering a well-thought-out **sermon** each Sunday. His preaching style was rather dry at first, but with experience and practice he soon began to move the hearts and spirits of his congregation.

FOR A LIST OF ORGANIZATIONS MENTIONED AND THEIR ABBREVIATIONS, SEE THE BOX ON PAGE 30.

Montgomery remained a completely **segregated** community; no attempt had been made to enforce the 1954 **Supreme Court** ruling on **integrated** education and none seemed likely. Only 2000 of the town's 40,000 **African Americans** were registered to vote, and few expected the situation to change. Elected to the executive committee of the local NAACP, King organized committees to help the poor and administer scholarship funds for high school graduates, but he was depressed by the size of the task facing him.

However, there were several personal highpoints at this time: the award of his **doctorate** in spring 1955, his growing friendship with local **minister** Ralph Abernathy, and the birth of his first child, Yolanda, in November.

The spark

On 1 December 1955, an incident occurred on a city bus which was to turn Montgomery, and eventually the whole nation, upside-down. African Americans were only allowed to sit in certain seats if no whites wanted them, but that evening a middle-aged African American seamstress named Rosa Parks refused to give up her seat when the driver ordered her to do so. She was arrested and charged with breaking the local bus **segregation** law.

▲ A Montgomery police officer takes Rosa Parks' fingerprints in February 1956. It was Rosa's refusal to give up her bus seat to a white passenger that triggered the Montgomery bus boycott.

On the buses

The rules governing bus travellers in Montgomery were highly complicated. Every bus was divided into three sections: the front rows for 'whites only', the back rows for African Americans, and the middle rows, which African Americans could occupy if no whites wanted to sit there. If a single white wanted to sit in one of the middle rows then all the African Americans in that row had to stand. African Americans had to buy their tickets from the driver (only whites were employed) at the front door, get off the bus, and re-enter at the back door, so as not to offend whites by walking through their section.

The African American community was enraged, and King invited ministers and other community leaders to meet in his church the next day. They decided to **boycott** (refuse to use) the city's buses from the following Monday. African American taxi firms agreed to take as many people as they could for the same 10-cent fare as the buses, and the rest were asked to walk. On Monday morning, the Kings, half expecting the boycott to fail, got up early to watch the first buses go past their house. They were empty.

The fire

That afternoon community leaders formed the Montgomery Improvement Association (MIA) to supervise the boycott, and King was elected president. In the evening he gave a moving speech to a huge crowd gathered in and around the Dexter Avenue church. He told the story of Rosa Parks' defiance, and he set it against the background of a whole people's suffering. He spoke simply but with great emotion. He asked people to remember those Christian and **democratic** values which were supposed to lie at the heart of the American dream. He acknowledged his people's anger, but he persuaded them not to sink to the level of their opponents.

YOU CAN LOCATE THE STATES AND TOWNS WHERE MARTIN LUTHER KING AND HIS FOLLOWERS WENT ON THE MAP ON PAGE 29.

His friend Abernathy read out the proposed demands: that drivers should treat African Americans with courtesy, that passengers should be seated on a first come, first served basis, and that African American drivers should also be employed. The crowd was unanimous in its agreement. Montgomery's African American community had found its cause and its leader. This, according to many historians, was the moment the American **civil rights** movement began.

The leader

There was no quick end to the Montgomery bus boycott.
The white authorities were determined to preserve
segregation, and believed surrender on the buses would lead
to surrender everywhere else. They fought back, outlawing the
use of taxis in place of the buses. The MIA responded by
forming a car pool, in which car-owners ran what was virtually
a free taxi service. Thousands continued to walk, and felt all
the better for it. One woman said that her feet might be tired,
but her soul was rested.

▼ *King addressing a mass meeting at Holt Street Baptist Church during
the Montgomery bus boycott, 22 March 1956.*

The eyes of America were focused on Montgomery, and King,
aged 26, was becoming a famous man. His press conferences
and speeches, full of eloquence, knowledge and idealism, were
something new, something America could not help responding
to. Much of that response was positive, but King quickly
became an object of hatred for those who saw their
segregated world under threat.

By early 1956 a trickle of threatening phone calls and mail had turned into a flood, and at the end of January King's house was bombed while he was out addressing a meeting. 'We cannot solve this problem through retaliatory violence,' he told the angry crowd who gathered outside. 'We must meet hate with love.'

Victory

The boycott dragged on through the spring and summer. The city authorities discovered an old law forbidding such actions, and brought King and 88 other community leaders to trial. They were found guilty, but appealed against that judgment and emerged from the trial looking more like heroes than villains. In desperation, the authorities tried to declare the car pool illegal. On 13 November they succeeded, but on the same day the Supreme Court in Washington finally ruled that Montgomery's bus segregation laws were **unconstitutional**. The protesters had won.

That night, 40 carloads of hooded and armed members of the racist **Ku Klux Klan** cruised through the African American neighbourhoods of Montgomery. They were trying to spread fear, but this time the residents refused to lock themselves away – they simply waved back. 'They acted as though they were watching a circus parade,' King wrote later.

On 21 December, King, Abernathy and other leaders were welcomed aboard a bus by a white driver. In the weeks to come there would be more incidents of white violence, and some said the only real change was the sharing of buses. Superficially they were right, but deep down everything had changed. African Americans had found their pride, their cause and their leader. King had proved that non-violence was a weapon that worked. There would be no going back.

▲ *Ralph Abernathy (left) and King (second left) are among the first to ride on Montgomery's newly integrated buses, 21 December 1956.*

Tired

'There comes a time when people get tired ... tired of being segregated and humiliated – tired of being kicked about by the brutal feet of oppression ... If we are wrong, the Supreme Court of this nation is wrong. If we are wrong, the Constitution of the United States is wrong. If we are wrong, God Almighty is wrong. If we are wrong, Jesus of Nazareth was merely a utopian dreamer who never came down to Earth. If we are wrong, justice is a lie.'

(From King's Dexter Avenue address on 5 December 1955)

Spreading the word

The success of the **boycott** in Montgomery encouraged similar actions in other Southern cities, and an organization called the Southern Christian Leadership Conference (SCLC) was formed to coordinate the protests. Martin Luther King became its first president.

White reaction to the victory in Montgomery was mixed. Some Southern state authorities began to stop **segregation**, but others dug in their heels, determined to resist. President Eisenhower would have preferred not to get involved, but that summer, in Little Rock, Arkansas, the authority of the **federal government** was deliberately challenged, and he was forced to intervene. When the Arkansas State Governor, in clear defiance of the **Supreme Court** ruling on **integration**, used national guard troops to prevent several **African American** students from starting at a local high school, Eisenhower sent in federal troops to secure their entry. The lesson of this episode – that the President took controversial action only when the cost of doing nothing looked even higher – was not lost on King.

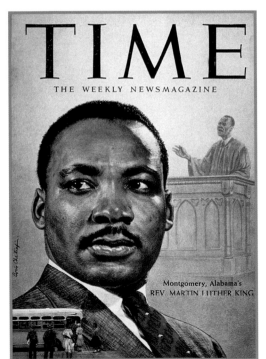

Friends and enemies

King's own fame continued to grow. His face appeared on the cover of *Time*, one of America's most important

◀ *King's portrait on the cover of* Time *magazine, recognizing the impact he was making across the country.*

news magazines, and he was asked to write a book, *Stride Toward Freedom*, about the bus boycott. In March, he and Coretta were invited to join independence celebrations in the new African state of Ghana.

Through 1957 and 1958 he toured and gave speeches, finished his book, and attended to his duties as **pastor** of Dexter Avenue Baptist Church and president of the SCLC.
In October 1957, Coretta gave birth to their first son, Martin Luther King III. King was overjoyed, but had little time to spend with the baby, or with the rest of his family. There was just too much work to do.

The more successful he was, the more enemies he had. White **racists** continued to harass him whenever they could, and on one occasion in 1958 he was arrested and beaten up by a particularly stupid policeman in front of a press photographer. King used his public trial to address the nation on the evils of the situation in **the South**.

Not all his enemies were white. The leaders of older African American organizations like NAACP and CORE were often jealous of King's success, while the more conservative African American church leaders felt threatened by his **radicalism**. At the other extreme, some younger African Americans, particularly in the North, were beginning to criticize King for his non-violent, 'love your enemy' approach. They wanted to overthrow 'white America', not plead for a greater share of it.

FOR A LIST OF ORGANIZATIONS MENTIONED AND THEIR ABBREVIATIONS, SEE THE BOX ON PAGE 30.

King's greatest ally outside the SCLC was the much older African American union leader A. Philip Randolph, whom he had long admired for his relentless promotion of African American rights.

Brush with death

Some enemies were more dangerous than others. On 20 September 1958, King was signing copies of *Stride Toward Freedom* in a New York bookstore when a middle-aged African American woman approached him. She asked him whether he was Martin Luther King, and when he said yes, she thrust a razor-sharp letter opener into his chest.

Dear Mr King

'I am a ninth grade student at the White Plains High School. While it shouldn't matter, I would like to mention that I am a white girl. I read in the paper of your misfortune and your suffering, and I read that if you had sneezed you would have died. I'm simply writing to say that I'm so happy you didn't sneeze.'

(Letter sent by a schoolgirl to King after his stabbing)

◀ *King with Coretta in a New York City Hospital, 10 days after being stabbed in a Harlem bookshop.*

At Harlem Hospital the doctors had to cut out a rib and part of his breastbone to remove the blade, which had narrowly missed his heart's main artery, the aorta. If King had sneezed, he would probably have bled to death.

When King learned the woman had mental health difficulties he refused to press charges: just 'get her healed,' he told the authorities.

Total commitment

King enjoyed his enforced rest: at last he had time for his family, and peace for reading and thought. In early 1959, he and Coretta visited India, where they prayed at the **shrine** of Gandhi (see 'Key people', page 58). They also had dinner with the Prime Minister, Gandhi's devoted friend Jawaharlal Nehru. Overall, King was greatly impressed with India, and particularly with the progress the country had made in the treatment of the **Untouchables**, those who had traditionally done the worst jobs in society. It was, he thought, time his own country showed itself equally willing to tackle the issue of segregation.

Back home, progress seemed agonizingly slow, and King decided he needed to increase his own level of commitment. With regret, he gave up his ministry in Montgomery and moved back to Atlanta, where he became the part-time co-pastor of his father's church. As 1959 unfolded, he and the other SCLC leaders took the decision to attack on a broad front, to push for **voter registration** and to challenge segregation wherever it raised its ugly head.

6 The struggle intensifies

YOU CAN LOCATE THE AREA KNOWN AS 'THE SOUTH' ON THE MAP ON PAGE 29.

King and the SCLC were not responsible for the next move in the struggle to free **the South**. In early February 1960, a group of **African American** students sat down at a **segregated** lunch counter in a Woolworth store in Greensboro, North Carolina, and refused to move until they were served. They were insulted and arrested. Within days **sit-ins** were spreading across the South, and the protests were front-page news across America. For the first time large numbers of African Americans were taking non-violent direct action in breach of the law. 'This is a new stage in the struggle,' one of King's closest colleagues, Stanley Levinson, wrote. 'It begins at the point where Montgomery left off'.

FOR A LIST OF ORGANIZATIONS MENTIONED AND THEIR ABBREVIATIONS, SEE THE BOX ON PAGE 30.

Delighted by this turn of events, King and the SCLC arranged a student conference that April in Raleigh, North Carolina. At the conference a new organization, the Student Non-violent Coordinating Committee (SNCC or 'Snick'), was born. For a few years the SNCC would operate as a younger, more impatient version of the SCLC, but by the mid-1960s, under the dynamic leadership of the young Stokely Carmichael, it would move away from non-violence and refuse to work with whites.

Time at home

That spring King had several problems to deal with. SCLC was, as usual, short of money, and fund-raising consumed a lot of his time. During February, a Montgomery court charged King with falsifying his tax returns in 1956–58.
This was a ridiculous charge to all who knew him, but many, King included, doubted whether he would receive a fair trial. He was both relieved and surprised when an all-white Southern jury found him innocent.

He was still spending a lot of his time on the road, and even home offered little refuge from work. 'We like to read and listen to music,' Coretta told a reporter from *Life* magazine, 'but we don't have time for it. We can't sit down to supper without somebody coming to the door. And the problems they bring Martin aren't always racial. Sometimes a man just wants to know how he can get his wife back.'

King worried that he was missing out on his children's growing up, and spent as much time playing with them as he could. He was not as strict as his own father had been, but insisted on smartness and good manners. That spring Coretta became pregnant. A second son, Dexter King, would be born in January 1961.

King and Kennedy

The sit-ins died out during the long summer holiday, but resumed in the autumn. King agreed to join one such protest in Atlanta that October and was arrested like everyone else. He was not, however, released with the others; the court decided he had broken the **probation** he had been given earlier that year for a minor traffic offence and was sentenced to four months' hard labour. Chained and handcuffed, King was driven to the Georgia State penitentiary and dumped in a small, cockroach-infested cell.

▲ *A handcuffed King is escorted from jail to court by two police officers, 25 October 1960. He had been arrested for taking part in an Atlanta department store sit-in.*

Four months earlier King had met Senator John F. Kennedy, one of the candidates for the **Democratic** presidential nomination that year. Kennedy did not particularly impress King at this first meeting, but Kennedy obviously realized King's support might help him win the election. When he heard of King's arrest, he phoned Coretta and told her he would try to help: two days later King was freed.

A few weeks later Kennedy won the presidential election by the narrowest of margins. Many historians believe that the African American votes he gained by helping King were decisive in his election.

When the two men met again, early in 1961, Kennedy was president. King was disappointed by how little Kennedy seemed prepared to do for African Americans, but took heart when the President told him that he liked a helpful push when it came to taking difficult decisions.

The Freedom Riders

The first major push was not given by SCLC, but by CORE. In the spring of 1961, CORE decided to put **Supreme Court** rulings banning segregation in inter-state travel to the test. A mixed group of African American and white people, calling themselves **Freedom Riders**, set out for New Orleans from Washington intent on sharing buses and conducting **sit-ins** at all the bus stations. In Alabama, one bus was set on fire, and when another reached the city of Birmingham the local police allowed members of the **racist** group **Ku Klux Klan** to beat the protesters with baseball bats and lead pipes. When more volunteers continued on to Montgomery they received a similar welcome.

King rushed to Montgomery to help, and was speaking in his friend Abernathy's church when it was attacked by a mob. A car was set on fire, and gas bombs thrown in through the shattered windows. Marshals of the **federal government** sent by the President's brother, **Attorney-General** Robert Kennedy, arrived in the nick of time.

Like the sit-ins, the Freedom Rides exposed the injustices of the South to the rest of America and the world. Their impact was limited – that same year King had to explain to his daughter why she could not visit a still-segregated amusement park in Atlanta – but they were successful. For most of the year SCLC had taken a back seat in favour of the students. Now it was King's turn for direct action.

▼ *Map showing the states known as 'the South'.*

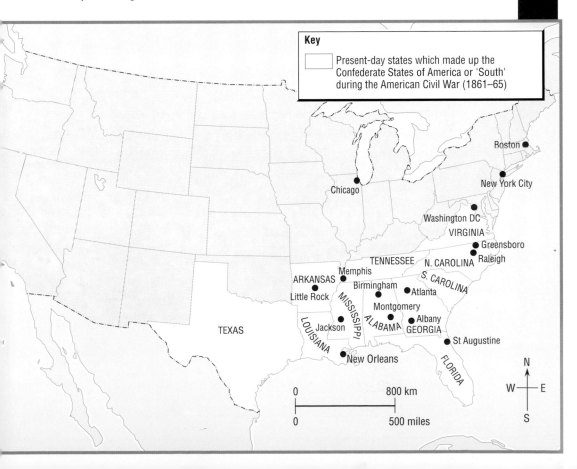

Key

☐ Present-day states which made up the Confederate States of America or 'South' during the American Civil War (1861–65)

Boston

New York City

Chicago

Washington DC

VIRGINIA

Greensboro

TENNESSEE   N. CAROLINA   Raleigh

Memphis

ARKANSAS   Birmingham   S. CAROLINA

Little Rock   MISSISSIPPI   Atlanta

Montgomery

TEXAS   LOUISIANA   Jackson   ALABAMA   Albany   GEORGIA

St Augustine

New Orleans   FLORIDA

N
W — E
S

0   800 km

0   500 miles

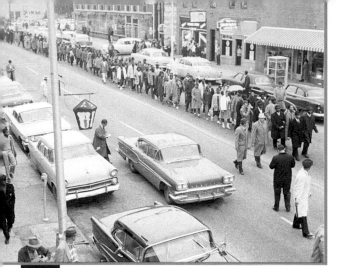

▲ *King leading protesters down a street in Albany, Georgia.*

Albany

In 1962, African American leaders in Albany, Georgia, asked for King's help with an anti-segregation campaign. However, the different African American groups – the SCLC, SNCC, NAACP – argued with each other, and the white authorities, although determined to retain segregation, were careful to do nothing that would upset the rest of America. Protesters were arrested, but without violence. When faced with the choice, the city preferred closing down facilities to integrating them. Slowly but surely the campaign fizzled out.

King learnt many lessons from this, his first real failure. Because whites formed the majority in most towns and counties in the South, African Americans could only triumph when the federal government was prepared to enforce **federal laws**. King was furious with the Kennedys for not intervening in Albany – he thought his campaign had given them a good enough excuse to do so. He now realized that they, like Eisenhower, needed more than an excuse. In 1963, he decided, he would give them more.

Abbreviations of civil rights organizations

CORE   Congress of Racial Equality
MIA   Montgomery Improvement Association
NAACP National Association for the Advancement of Colored People
SCLC   Southern Christian Leadership Conference
SNCC   Student Non-violent Coordinating Committee

For his next campaign King chose Birmingham, Alabama, which many believed was the most **racist** city in **the South**. There had recently been an attempt to ban **African American** music from the local radio stations, and a children's book featuring black and white rabbits had been banned. The African American population lived in constant fear of white violence; the city's police chief was Eugene 'Bull' Connor, a brutal and foul-mouthed racist. Behind him stood newly elected State Governor George Wallace, whose slogan was '**Segregation** now, segregation tomorrow, segregation forever'. These men, King believed, would make ideal opponents.

YOU CAN LOCATE THE AREA KNOWN AS 'THE SOUTH' ON THE MAP ON PAGE 29.

Marching to jail

King and his colleagues, mindful of the failure in Albany, planned the Birmingham campaign with great care. It was decided that rather than challenge the city authorities directly, they would target the more vulnerable business community. As few African Americans had the vote, their political power was limited, but a campaign of **sit-ins**, **boycotts** and mass marches could seriously damage the city's big department stores.

Pain for gain

'We must say to our white brothers all over the South who try to keep us down: We will match your capacity to inflict suffering with our capacity to endure suffering.'

(King, speaking in Birmingham, 1963)

The campaign began in early April, a few days after the birth of King's second daughter, Bernice. A **manifesto** listed the SCLC's demands: integrated lunch counters, toilets and drinking fountains; more jobs for African Americans in local business; the establishment of a mixed black and white committee to oversee general **desegregation**. Sit-ins, boycotts and marches began, and by the end of the first week some 300 were in jail. On 12 April, King joined one of the marches, and was also arrested.

While in jail, King read a newspaper article in which white churchmen criticized him for being too impatient, for breaking the law, and for generally being too 'extreme'. An angry King wrote a long reply on anything he could find – from scraps of paper bags to toilet paper – clearly explaining and passionately defending his actions. This 'Letter from Birmingham Jail' became a classic document of the **civil rights** movement.

Prison thoughts

'Abused and scorned though we may be, our destiny is tied up with America's destiny. Before the pilgrims landed at Plymouth, we were here. Before the pen of Jefferson etched the majestic words of the Declaration of Independence across the pages of history, we were here. For more than two centuries our forebears laboured in this country without wages ... If the inexpressible cruelties of slavery could not stop us, the oppression we now face will surely fail.'

(From King's 'Letter from Birmingham Jail')

Children's crusade

When King was released towards the end of April, he found that the protests were failing for lack of volunteers. One colleague suggested that they use schoolchildren to swell the numbers, and, although doubtful at first, King eventually agreed. At the beginning of May, over 1000 children, aged 6 and over, took part in a mass march. Nine hundred were arrested. One police officer angrily asked an eight-year-old girl what she wanted. 'Freedom,' she replied.

On the following day more than 2500 children marched, and something snapped in Bull Connor. When the marchers refused to retrace their steps, he told his men to 'let them have it'. High-pressure water from fire hoses knocked children down and threw them into walls. When bystanders retaliated by throwing bottles, Connor unleashed police dogs trained to attack and many children were badly bitten. 'Look at those niggers run,' he sneered.

▼ *A police dog attacks a 17-year-old protester during the Birmingham civil rights protest, 3 May 1963.*

▲ A close-up of Attorney General Robert Kennedy and President John F. Kennedy, taken during the Birmingham protests.

The television cameras carried the images of violence around the world. Most Americans were horrified. Within two days, Robert Kennedy's assistant Burke Marshall was on his way to Birmingham with instructions to force the city's businessmen into a deal. In Washington President Kennedy was planning a new and much tougher Civil Rights Bill.

Meanwhile, the demonstrations went on, and on 5 May a group of black churchmen led a march into the city centre. When they reached Connor's police line they were told to turn back. 'We have done nothing wrong,' the Reverend Billups said. 'All we want is our freedom. Bring on your dogs. Beat us up. Turn on your hoses. We are not going to retreat.'

Connor ordered his men to turn on their hoses. They ignored him, and stood aside, some with tears streaming down their cheeks, to let the protesters pass. 'I saw there the pride and the power of non-violence,' King said later.

Five days later an agreement was reached. The businessmen of Birmingham accepted almost all of the SCLC's demands. King had won another great victory.

8 Dreams and nightmares

The events in Birmingham persuaded President Kennedy of the need for drastic action. 'Are we to say to the world, and much more importantly to each other,' he asked a national TV audience on 11 June 1963, 'that this is the land of the free except for the Negroes [**African Americans**], that we have no second class citizens except the Negroes …' Five days later he submitted a new far-reaching **Civil Rights** Bill to **Congress**.

But would it ever become law? On the day that Kennedy addressed the nation, civil rights leader Medgar Evers was shot down by white **racists** in front of his house in Jackson, Mississippi. There was strong opposition to reform, and African Americans knew it. Through the summer of 1963 the protests went on growing in size and number. Across **the South**, 100 cities witnessed nearly 1000 demonstrations of one sort or another and more than 20,000 people were arrested.

YOU CAN LOCATE THE AREA KNOWN AS 'THE SOUTH' ON THE MAP ON PAGE 29.

King travelled 440,000 kilometres (275,0000 miles) and gave 350 speeches in 1963, and everywhere he went he was surrounded by people asking for his autograph. He had not suffered the way so many of his fellow African Americans had, and felt undeserving of such adulation. He was a humble man, and more than ready to laugh at himself. He particularly enjoyed the story of one 'big Negro guy' who stood up to a rude white bus driver with the words: 'one, I ain't no boy [a derogatory term for black men], and two, I ain't one of those Martin Luther King non-violent Negroes.'

Washington and after
In the aftermath of Birmingham it was decided that a mass march on Washington would be a good way of putting pressure on Congress to pass the Civil Rights Bill. Although not much involved in the planning, King agreed to speak at the rally.

The organizers were hoping for 100,000 people at the rally, but were overjoyed to find a quarter of a million campaigners, both black and white, gathered in front of the Lincoln Memorial on 28 August. There were many speeches – each speaker was limited to eight minutes – but King's address, with its haunting repetition of the phrase 'I have a dream', was the one that everyone would remember.

The dreamer

'I say to you today, my friends, that in spite of the difficulties and frustrations of the moment I still have a dream. It is a dream deeply rooted in the American dream.

'I have a dream that one day this nation will rise up and live out the true meaning of its creed: "We hold these truths to be self-evident – that all men are created equal."

'I have a dream that one day on the red hills of Georgia the sons of former slaves and former slave owners will be able to sit down together at the table of brotherhood.

'I have a dream that one day even the state of Mississippi, a desert state sweltering with the heat of injustice and oppression, will be transformed into an oasis of freedom and justice.

'I have a dream that my four little children will one day live in a nation where they will not be judged by the colour of their skin but by the content of their character.

'I have a dream today.'

(From King's famous speech to the
Washington rally, 28 August 1963)

▲ *King giving the 'I have a dream' speech in Washington DC,
28 August 1963.*

The march was a tremendous success, and King was near the
peak of his popularity, but the obstacles to further progress
remained enormous. The well-publicized bombing of a church
in Birmingham a few weeks later, which took the lives of four
young girls, was only one of many violent attacks committed
that autumn by angry whites. The assassination of Kennedy in
November was a personal blow to King, who had eventually
come to admire the young President, but he also saw it as a
victory for the 'climate of hate' which seemed to be taking
over America. He thought his own chances of meeting a
similar fate were high. 'I don't think I'm going to live to reach
40,' he told Coretta.

▲ *Malcolm X, chief spokesman for the Nation of Islam between 1958 and 1964.*

Black power?

King might have expected opposition and threats from white extremists and the white establishment in Washington – the **FBI** continued to harass him and the other SCLC leaders, secretly recording their private phone calls and conversations in hotel rooms – but he was less prepared for the obstacles now being placed in his path by critical African Americans. The **Nation of Islam** leader Malcolm X was more outspoken than most, but his criticisms of King did reflect widespread feelings among younger African American activists, particularly in northern states.

King, they said, was an ideal African American leader for whites because he believed in America – he was always talking about the constitution, the Declaration of Independence, the American Dream – but he asked for only limited reform. He ignored the real issues confronting African Americans, which was their place in the economic system, and the poverty that they lived in.

King was aware of these criticisms – he even agreed with many of them – but he rejected the solutions which Malcolm X and the more **radical** leaders of the SNCC proposed. He thought their calls for violent resistance were both morally wrong and deeply impractical

Martin and Malcolm X

The Southern-born Martin wanted to integrate American society; the Northern-born Malcolm wanted nothing to do with whites for most of his adult life. Martin insisted on non-violence, which Malcolm rejected, but Malcolm only ever recommended using violence in self-defence. Both men were passionate fighters for their people.

King also knew that a white failure to improve the lives of African Americans would only strengthen the hand of those who believed in violence.

A break for applause

With Congress reluctant to defy the wishes of the murdered Kennedy, a determined push from the new President Johnson ensured the passing of the Civil Rights bill in June 1964. The South's 'Jim Crow' laws were finally dismantled.

Late in the year it was announced that King had won the **Nobel Peace Prize**, and in December he travelled to Oslo to receive the award. He spoke there of his 'abiding faith' in his own country, but he also knew that the battle was far from over. Most African Americans in the South still lacked the vote and that summer several **ghettos** in Northern states had exploded in murderous riots. The dream could still turn into a nightmare.

▶ *King with the Nobel Prize he was awarded in 1964.*

9 Securing the vote

YOU CAN LOCATE THE AREA KNOWN AS 'THE SOUTH' ON THE MAP ON PAGE 29.

Before turning his attention to the North, King had one last task to accomplish in **the South**. A century had passed since the end of slavery, but few **African Americans** in the South were registered to vote. When they tried to do so they were turned down for the most ridiculous reasons, like a failure to cross a 't' or the use of an initial instead of a middle name. Those who filled in the form correctly were set impossible tasks, like reciting an obscure state law from memory. A Voting Rights Bill was needed to stop such practices, but late in 1964 President Johnson told King there was little hope that **Congress** would agree to one so soon after passing the **Civil Rights** Bill.

◀ *African Americans in Hernando, Mississippi. King campaigned for the right of African Americans to register to vote in small towns like this throughout the American South.*

Selma, Alabama

King decided that Johnson, like Kennedy before him, needed a 'push'. He and his colleagues decided to mount a **voter registration** campaign in the small town of Selma, Alabama. The local police chief, Sheriff Clark, was a crude and violent **racist**, and most of his deputies were members of the **Ku Klux Klan**. Like Bull Connor, he would make a wonderfully obvious enemy.

The campaign swung into action on 18 January 1965, when several small groups of African Americans walked to the town courthouse and asked to be registered to vote. They were turned away. Next day, and the day after that, more arrived with the same request, and Sheriff Clark lost his patience. Wearing a prominent 'Never' badge, he beat one woman with a club right in front of watching TV cameras.

Things were going as King had expected. On 31 January he joined a march to the courthouse, was arrested, and joined the swelling number in jail. There he composed another famous letter. 'This is Selma, Alabama,' he wrote. 'There are more Negroes in jail with me than there are on the voting rolls.'

Marching on Montgomery

The authorities reacted with increasing violence. Clark and his deputies used electric prods on one group of students, and a night march was ambushed by state troopers. One young man, Jimmie Lee Jackson, was shot in the stomach by a trooper for trying to defend his mother and grandfather.

King decided he would lead a march to the state capital Montgomery, some 80 kilometres (50 miles) away, to petition the State Governor, George Wallace. On the agreed date, however, King was busy in Atlanta, and it was decided that the march would start without him. Outside Selma, on Highway 80, the marchers found themselves face-to-face with an army of state troopers. They were ordered to turn back, but before they could, the troopers were amongst them, hitting out with clubs. A tear-gas attack forced a retreat, and then they were ambushed by Clark and his deputies swinging bullwhips and rubber tubes wrapped in barbed wire. Seventy African Americans were hospitalized; it was a miracle none died.

King, full of guilt for not being there, appealed to religious leaders all over America to join him for another march. The response was tremendous, and churchmen of all races and religions were soon arriving in Selma. While they were waiting for official permission to march, James Reeb, a white **Unitarian minister** from Boston, was beaten to death by a bunch of young white thugs.

▲ *An official White House portrait of President Lyndon B. Johnson in 1964.*

This white death provoked a storm of anger across America, and Johnson was finally provoked into introducing a Voting Rights Bill. 'Their cause must be our cause too,' he told the nation. 'Because it's not just Negroes, but really it's all of us who must overcome the crippling legacy of bigotry and injustice. And,' he added, deliberately repeating the words of the civil rights hymn, 'we shall overcome!' King, watching on TV, found himself in tears.

Full circle

A new march to Montgomery set out on 21 March, and arrived four days later outside Governor Wallace's statehouse, where a crowd of 25,000 heard King deliver another of his many memorable speeches. What he sought was 'a society at peace with itself, a society that can live with its conscience. That will be a day not of the white man, not of the black man. That will be the day of man as man.'

The legal battles had mostly been won. **Economic discrimination** against African Americans was now the main issue, and it was to this that King would turn his attention.

▲ *Civil rights marchers leave Selma, Alabama, for Montgomery, 21 March 1965. In 1966, the US Congress designated this 80 kilometres (50 miles) of road as a 'national historic trail'.*

Key dates of the Civil Rights struggle

1955	• December	Montgomery bus boycott begins
1960	• February	Student **sit-ins** begin
1961	• May	The **Freedom Rides**
1963	• April–May	The campaign in Birmingham
	• August	March on Washington
1964	• July	Kennedy's second **Civil Rights** Bill
1965	• Jan–March	Campaign in Selma and march to Montgomery
	• August	Voting Rights Bill

By the mid-1960s roughly 60 per cent of **African Americans** lived outside the old **South**, mostly in the large cities of the north, east and west. There was no web of laws to keep them in an unequal position, but most of them were little or no better off than their Southern brothers and sisters. **Segregation** in housing and education, though not legally enforced, was just as real. Most African Americans lived in **ghettos**, where they went to poor schools and lived in poor housing. They were much more likely to be unemployed, and the jobs they had were often those which whites did not want to do. Crime was a daily fact of life, policing either brutal or non-existent.

King had thought that his campaigns in the South would help African Americans in the rest of the country, but by 1965 he was not so sure. The changes had come too slowly, and the urban riots of the previous year proved only the first in a series of what he called 'long, hot summers'. In 1965, the Los Angeles ghetto of Watts exploded into violence; 34 died and 4000 were arrested. King, while condemning the violence, understood what had caused it. America, he believed, had to do something to help its urban poor.

YOU CAN SEE THE STATES AND TOWNS WHERE MARTIN LUTHER KING AND HIS FOLLOWERS WENT ON THE MAP ON PAGE 29.

Chicago

He chose Chicago, then America's second city, for his major campaign of 1966. Conditions for African Americans were as bad there as anywhere, and the local **civil rights** organizations seemed strong and well-organized. He knew the city would be a tough nut to crack, but was cautiously optimistic.

Despite careful preparation – King's workers tirelessly visited home after home in the **slum** neighbourhoods, asking people what they most needed – the campaign never really gathered momentum. A series of strikes and **boycotts** were supposed to set the stage for mass direct action, but money ran short, the various groups began arguing with each other, and the mass of the African American population seemed unwilling to get involved.

▲ King and his wife Coretta in the Chicago four-room slum apartment they took as their home for several months in early 1966. King said living there was the only way he could truly understand the problems of slum life.

The only real success was 'Operation Breadbasket', an employment creation programme run by one of King's local disciples, the young Jesse Jackson. By the end of the year, King was thoroughly depressed: it had become increasingly clear to him that **racism** had deeper roots than he had previously suspected. It was more than just ignorance and prejudice; it reinforced a whole system of economic **exploitation**. The ghettos were white America's **colonies** inside the USA.

SCLC's success in the South, he now realized, had been possible because they had not threatened the system as a whole.

A revolution of values

'For years I laboured with the idea of reforming the existing institutions of the South, a little change here, a little change there. Now I feel quite differently. I think you've got to have a reconstruction of the whole society, a revolution of values.'

(King, talking to journalist David Halberstam, spring 1967)

At college he had wondered out loud about the fairness of **capitalism**, and now he did so again. 'Something is wrong with the economic system of our nation,' he said; there had to be **redistribution of wealth**. In private he spoke of his admiration for Sweden's system of **democratic socialism**, but agreed that America was not ready to hear about such things just yet.

The War

During this period another issue was deeply concerning King. The USA had been involved in the small South-east Asian country of Vietnam for over a decade, but in 1964–65 that involvement mushroomed into a full-scale war. By the summer of 1965, 125,000 US troops were fighting in Vietnam, and this figure would more than treble over the next two years.

▲ *US ground troops in Vietnam, November 1967.*

King opposed the war for several reasons. He was concerned that Vietnam was a corrupt **dictatorship** and did not think the USA should support such governments. He was appalled by the use of cruel weapons like **napalm**. He resented the fact that African Americans were being called up to fight in large numbers even though they were a small proportion of the American population. He was also angry that money which might have been spent on reducing poverty at home was being wasted on such a war.

In early 1967, in a speech at the Riverside Church in New York, he finally expressed the completeness of his opposition. Colleagues had told him not to mix civil rights and Vietnam, and he knew it was politically unwise to do so, but he felt that 'someone of influence has to say the US is wrong, and everybody is afraid to say it'.

Vietnam

'We were taking the black young men who had been crippled by our society and sending them 8000 miles away to guarantee liberties in south-east Asia which they had not found in south-west Georgia and East Harlem. So we have been repeatedly faced with the cruel irony of watching Negro and white boys on TV screens as they kill and die together for a nation that has been unable to seat them together in the same schools ... I could not be silent in the face of such cruel manipulation of the poor.'

'Somehow this madness must cease. We must stop now. I speak as a child of God and brother to the suffering poor of Vietnam. I speak for those whose land is being laid waste, whose homes are being destroyed, whose culture is being subverted ...'

(From King's address at the Riverside Church, New York City, 4 April 1967)

As his colleagues had feared, the criticism rained down on King's head. The *New York Times* accused him of '**whitewashing** Hanoi'; the *Washington Post* of reducing 'his usefulness to his cause, his country, and to his people'. Lyndon Johnson was outraged; **FBI** documents called him 'a traitor to his country and his race'. King, though upset by the press criticism, made no apologies. 'I will not stand by,' he said, 'when I see an unjust war taking place.'

Death in Memphis

King had first heard the slogan 'black power' from SNCC activists on a march through Mississippi in 1966, and had instantly disliked it. It suggested both violence and **separatism**, whereas he had always fought for non-violence and **integration**. The **glamorization**, if not practice, of violent revolution by various 'black power' groups made King's more demanding, peaceful methods seem less appealing. With the Vietnam War raging and cities burning, how could **African Americans** 'love their enemies'?

FOR A LIST OF ORGANIZATIONS MENTIONED AND THEIR ABBREVIATIONS, SEE THE BOX ON PAGE 30.

By the end of 1967 the **civil rights** movement had virtually disintegrated. King had lost the support of many African American **radicals**, and his assault on the establishment over poverty and Vietnam had lost him the support of many whites and African American moderates.

Home was no longer the refuge it had been. His children gave him great joy, but his relationship with Coretta was strained. King had several affairs with other women and Coretta's resentment was made worse by his insistence that she remain a traditional housewife, with little independent life of her own.

▲ Cover of a pamphlet circulated by the SNCC in the summer of 1967.

The Poor People's March

Close to despair, King came up with one last great idea: a Poor People's March on the nation's capital. By putting economic circumstances before race he would challenge the very notion of 'black power'.

This was a march for all America's less fortunate people, whether they were members of oppressed ethnic minorities like the African Americans, Hispanic Americans and Native Americans, or the poorest whites. King was moving beyond race and racial politics. By mounting a sustained campaign of **civil disobedience** in the seat of American government, King hoped to 'cripple the operations of an oppressive society.' It was, he said, 'a "last chance" project to arouse the American conscience.'

Not surprisingly the idea provoked opposition from all sides. Moderate African Americans thought he had given in to radicals, while radicals thought he had sold out his own race. Whites worried that Washington would end up in flames. One letter to President Johnson advised him to 'lock up Martin Luther King or we will have a social revolution.'

Memphis

In early March, six weeks before the planned Poor People's March, King received a request for help from Memphis, Tennessee. Rubbish collectors campaigning for union recognition and better pay had been assaulted by police, and the city's African American community closed ranks behind them. Now they needed King's support.

King and his assistants arrived on 18 March. They checked into the Lorraine Motel, in central Memphis, where King had always stayed, and that evening he addressed a large and passionate congregation at the Mason Temple. He agreed to lead a march during the following week, but when the day came gangs of youths started smashing windows and looting shops. King called off the march immediately, saying he would have no part in violence, but the situation was already out of control. Sixty people were injured, many shops damaged, and one young man was shot dead by the police.

King flew home to Atlanta, but knew he could not simply abandon Memphis. He was determined to lead a non-violent march there, if only to show he could lead one in Washington. Against the wishes of his aides he flew back to Memphis on 3 April, and that evening gave his last address – one that seemed to anticipate his own death.

The promised land

'It really doesn't matter with me now. Because I have been to the mountaintop. ... And I've looked over. And I've seen the promised land. I may not get there with you. But I want you to know tonight that we as a people will get to the promised land. So I'm happy tonight. I'm not worried about anything. I'm not fearing any man. Mine eyes have seen the glory of the coming of the Lord!'

(From King's address at the Mason Temple, Memphis, 3 April 1968)

▲ *King standing on the balcony of the Lorraine Motel, Memphis, 3 April 1968. The following day he was standing roughly in the same spot when he was shot and killed. From left: Hosea Williams, Jesse Jackson, King and Ralph Abernathy.*

The following evening King was standing on the balcony of the Lorraine Motel when a bullet shot from a high-powered rifle tore away half his neck and jaw. Rushed to hospital, he was pronounced dead an hour later. He was nine months short of his 40th birthday.

Free at last

His death sparked angry riots across the country. Like Gandhi, whom he had so admired, King was laid to rest amidst outbreaks of the violence he had so hated in life. His friend Abernathy, who had been at his side since the early days in Montgomery, officiated at the funeral in Atlanta. There were 800 people inside Ebenezer Church, and 60,000 outside.

King was buried beside his beloved grandmother. On the crypt were carved lines from the end of his 'I have a dream' speech in Washington: 'Free at last, free at last, thank God almighty, I'm free at last'.

▼ *The mahogany casket containing King's body is drawn by mules through the streets of Atlanta, 9 April 1968.*

Legacy

The system of legalized **racism** which existed in the American **South** between the end of slavery and the 1960s was not only unjust, it was also out of step with the rest of American society. A successful **civil rights** movement in some shape or form was bound to happen, with or without Martin Luther King Jr.

YOU CAN LOCATE THE AREA KNOWN AS 'THE SOUTH' ON THE MAP ON PAGE 29.

Nevertheless, he provided that movement with a style, an emphasis and a level of imagination which was all his own. As a speaker he was unsurpassed; as a political organizer he gave the struggle a religious sense of morality – of right and wrong – which proved both inspiring and effective. He learned quickly from his few failures, and was usually imaginative enough to keep his opponents on the wrong foot. The crucial campaigns of the civil rights movement in the South are hard to imagine without him.

▶ *The statue of Martin Luther King Jr. at Westminster Abbey in London, a memorial to his struggle on behalf of persecuted and oppressed people of the world.*

KING

A true revolutionary

Outside the South King was less successful. However, it should be stressed that the size of the task here was so much greater and he had much less time to make a difference. Only two years passed between the beginning of his campaign in Chicago and his assassination.

King's critics among the more **radical** African American groups argued that his non-violent methods were self-limiting. White America could afford to give way in the South because the repeal of 'Jim Crow' laws did not threaten the system as a whole, but an attack on African American poverty did threaten the system. Outside the South, King's appeal to white consciences would inevitably fall on deaf ears.

In the short run, at least, these critics were proved correct, and by the time of his death King himself had come to believe that the problems of race and poverty in America could only be solved by a radical overhaul of American **capitalism**. In this respect he was every bit as revolutionary as Malcolm X, who is so often contrasted with him.

When it came to methods, however, the difference remained. King realized his methods were unlikely to work quickly, but he doubted whether his opponents' methods would work at all. Against the might of the American establishment, he thought, campaigns of violence were doomed to failure. 'Black power' might be inspirational as an idea, but as a political programme it was little more than a dangerous fantasy.

An inspiration

The experience of African Americans since King's death has borne out much of his later pessimism.

A committed life

'Say that I was a drum major for justice. Say that I was a drum major for peace. That I was a drum major for righteousness. And all of the shallow things will not matter. I won't have any money to leave behind. I won't have the fine and luxurious things of life to leave behind. But I just want to leave a committed life behind. And that's all I want to say...'

(From King's last sermon, 4 February 1968)

The legal limitations on full African American participation in the wider society have mostly been removed, but racism remains a powerfully divisive force. A significant African American middle class has come into being, but most African Americans still suffer from **economic discrimination**. On the day before his death King told a Memphis congregation that 'we as a people will get to the promised land', but early in the 21st century there still seems some way to go.

Since 1983, 15 January has been celebrated in the USA as Martin Luther King Jr. Day. However, the man remembered on that day is rarely the anti-racist, anti-war, anti-poverty King of his final years, the man who stressed how much still needed to change. He is presented instead as the victor of the civil rights campaign, the proof that American **democracy** works, the happy ending to a sad story. King's achievements as a civil rights leader in the South were certainly monumental, but to characterize the breadth of his beliefs and achievements in such a limited way does him and the world a great disservice.

At heart, King was a fighter against injustice. Like Gandhi, he did not want his own people to become like their oppressors. On the contrary, he hoped that by appealing non-violently to the consciences of their enemies they might inspire a better world for everyone. 'If we protest courageously, and yet with dignity and Christian love,' he said early in the Montgomery bus boycott, 'then when the history books are written in the future, somebody will have to say, "There lived a race of people, of black people, of people who had the moral courage to stand up for their rights. And thereby they injected a new meaning into the veins of history and civilization".'

▼ *A single flower rests on the tomb of Martin Luther King Jr. in Atlanta, Georgia.*

REV. MARTIN LUTHER KING, JR.
1929 — 1968

"Free at last, Free at last,
Thank God Almighty
I'm Free at last."

Timeline

1929	Martin Luther King Jr. born 15 January, in Atlanta, Georgia
1944	Enters Morehouse College, Atlanta
1947	**Ordained** at Ebenezer Baptist Church, Atlanta
1948	Enrols at Crozer Theological Seminary, Pennsylvania
1951	Enters Boston University School of Theology
1953	Marries Coretta Scott in Marion, Alabama
1954	**Supreme Court** rules that **segregated** schooling is illegal
	King becomes **pastor** of Dexter Avenue Baptist Church
1955	Montgomery bus **boycott** begins (5 December)
	Birth of first child Yolanda (November)
1956	Boycott continues; King jailed for the first time
	Montgomery buses **integrated**
1957	Establishment of SCLC
	King visits Ghana
	Birth of second child Martin (October)
1958	Writes *Stride Toward Freedom*
	Survives knife attack in Harlem, New York
1959	Visits India
1960	Student **sit-in** movement begins (SNCC formed)
1961	'**Freedom Rides**' through **the South**
	Birth of third child Dexter (January)
1963	Birth of fourth child Bernice (March)
	King leads successful campaign in Birmingham (April–May)
	Gives 'I have a dream' speech in Washington (28 August)
	Assassination of President Kennedy (22 November)
1964	**Civil Rights** Act passed (July)
	King awarded **Nobel Peace Prize**
1965	Leads campaign in Selma, Alabama
	March on Montgomery
	Voting Rights Act passed (August)
	Riots in Watts district of Los Angeles, California
1966	King leads campaign in Chicago
1967	Gives major speech condemning the war in Vietnam
	Summer of riots in many cities
	King announces Poor People's Campaign
1968	Leads march in Memphis supporting employment rights
	Martin Luther King Jr. assassinated in Memphis (4 April)

FOR A LIST OF ORGANIZATIONS MENTIONED AND THEIR ABBREVIATIONS SEE THE BOX ON PAGE 30.

Key people of King's time

Ralph Abernathy (1926–90) became friends with King in Montgomery, where both men were politically active church **pastors**. Served as King's right-hand-man in the Southern Christian Leadership Conference (SCLC) and through all the major campaigns. After King's death he took over as president of the SCLC until 1977.

Dwight D. Eisenhower (1890–1969) was US President from 1953 to 1969. He was reluctant to involve the **federal government** in racial matters, but in 1957 the State of Arkansas' refusal to allow black student registration at a college in Little Rock forced him to impose **federal law** using federal troops.

Mohandas Gandhi (1869–1948) was an Indian nationalist leader in both South Africa (1893–1914) and India (1915–48). A deeply religious man, he pioneered the techniques of non-violent protest and **civil disobedience** that Martin Luther King Jr. used to such effect in the **civil rights** struggle.

Jesse Jackson (1941–) joined King's SCLC staff in Chicago as a young clergymen, and ran the successful job campaign Operation Breadbasket. By the beginning of the 1980s he was perhaps the most prominent **African American** political leader. In both 1984 and 1988 he sought but failed to secure the **Democratic** presidential nomination.

Lyndon B. Johnson (1908–73) became Vice-President when John F. Kennedy was elected President in 1960. As Vice-President, he automatically became President when Kennedy was assassinated in November 1963. He steered Kennedy's second Civil Rights Bill through **Congress** in 1964. In 1965 he forced through the Voting Rights Bill, but his ambitious social programme was undercut by his determination to win the Vietnam War. The growing unpopularity of the war was the main reason for his decision not to stand for re-election in 1968.

John F. Kennedy (1917–63) spent fourteen years in Congress before being elected President in November 1960. He supported civil rights for African Americans. He believed, however, that concentration on this one issue would cost him his majorities in Congress, and prevent him from succeeding in areas he considered just as important. Consequently, his early civil rights measures were half-hearted. He was finally forced to establish civil rights by African American pressure and his awakening conscience. He was assassinated in November 1963, but his Civil Rights Bill became law under his successor Lyndon Johnson.

Robert F. Kennedy (1925–68) was appointed **Attorney-General** by his older brother John F. Kennedy in 1960, and held the post until 1964. His forcefully stated willingness to enforce federal laws and use federal troops contributed to the successes of the Freedom Riders and King's campaign in Birmingham, Alabama. After his brother's death he, like King, became an increasingly outspoken critic of the Vietnam War. He was assassinated in 1968, while campaigning for that year's Democratic presidential nomination.

Malcolm X (born Malcolm Little) (1925–65) became chief spokesman for the Black Muslims (the **Nation of Islam**) in 1958. A campaigner for African American rights, he argued for separate African American development, advocated the use of violence in self-defence, and criticized the more cooperative approach taken by campaigners like King. In 1964, he split from the Nation of Islam and moderated his views on **separatism** and violence. He was assassinated in 1965.

A. Philip Randolph (1889–1979) was a trade union leader and civil rights activist for over 50 years. He was the founding father of the first African American trade union, the Brotherhood of Sleeping Car Porters, and helped to persuade President Truman to **desegregate** the US Armed Forces in 1948. He was one of the organizers of the march on Washington in 1963.

Further reading & other resources

Further reading

Long Walk to Freedom, Nelson Mandela, Abacus Books, 1994
Malcolm X, David Downing, Heinemann Library, 2002
Martin Luther King, John Malam, Evans, 1999
The Story of Martin Luther King, James Riordan, Belitha, 2001
To Kill a Mockingbird, Harper Lee, Pan, 1974

Sources and acknowledgements

The publishers would like to thank the following for permission to reproduce copyright material from:
Bearing the Cross: Martin Luther King Jr. and the Southern Christian Leadership Conference, David Garrow, Jonathan Cape/Vintage, 1993. Reprinted by permission of the Random House Group Ltd.
Let the Trumpet Sound: The Life of Martin Luther King Jr., Stephen B. Oates, Mentor, 1985
Martin Luther King Jr., Nancy Shuker, Burke, 1988

Websites

National Park Service website: www.nps.gov/malu
Website of the King Centre, established by Coretta Scott King in 1968: www.thekingcentre.org
US Holidays on the Net website: www.holidays.net/mlk

Films

To Kill a Mockingbird (based on the novel by Harper Lee, starring Gregory Peck and Mary Badham, directed by Robert Mulligan, 1962)
Malcolm X (starring Denzel Washington, directed by Spike Lee, 1992)
Mississippi Burning (starring Gene Hackman and Willem Dafoe, directed by Alan Parker, 1988)

Glossary

African American in the USA, American with African ancestors. During King's lifetime the words 'coloured', 'negro' and 'black' were also used by this community to describe itself. The word 'nigger' was used by whites as a racial insult.

Attorney-General chief legal official of the US

bigotry unreasonable prejudice and intolerance

boycott refusal to have any dealings with a business firm or other institution

capitalism economic system in which the production and distribution of goods depend on private wealth and profit

civil disobedience peaceful form of protest usually involving the refusal to obey particular laws or to pay particular taxes

civil rights legal rights of all people to the same equal opportunities and benefits

colonialism policy of getting and ruling colonies – territories run by another, usually faraway, country

Congress the law-making arm of the US government, comprising the Senate and the House of Representatives

democratic taking account of the wishes of the whole population

desegregation see segregation

dictatorship government by an individual (called a dictator) who denies the people any say in decision-making

doctorate highest university degree, abbreviated as PhD

economic discrimination unfair treatment in matters relating to the economy (e.g. work availability, housing)

exploitation making use of, often unfairly or selfishly

FBI in the USA, Federal Bureau of Investigation. It investigates crimes that may affect security in the country.

federal government in the USA, the central government based in Washington, DC

federal laws laws made by the federal government, which must be observed throughout the USA, and which override state laws

Freedom Riders organized group of civil rights protesters who set out to test the laws applying to racial integration on interstate public transport in 1961

ghetto part of a city, usually a poor part, mostly occupied by a minority group

glamorization making something look attractive and exciting

integration bringing together, breaking down barriers. In racial matters, integration is the opposite of segregation.

Ku Klux Klan racist society formed after the American Civil War with the aim of maintaining white supremacy. Famous for its white hoods and burning crosses, it was responsible for hanging and killing hundreds of African Americans.

manifesto list of intended political actions

minister clergyman in the Christian church

napalm jellied petrol which bursts into flame on impact

Nation of Islam African American separatist organization founded in the early 1930s by Wallace Fard Muhammad, and subsequently led by Elijah Muhammad

Nobel Peace Prize annual international prize awarded for outstanding achievements in securing peace

ordained accepted as a minister

pastor person in charge of a church

probation period in which offender risks going to prison if he breaks any of the accompanying rules

racial discrimination treating people badly because they belong to a particular racial group

racism (racist) treating individuals or groups differently (and usually worse) just because they belong to a different race.

radicalism belief in far-reaching change

redistribution of wealth making richer people poorer to make poorer people richer

segregation in racial matters, the enforced separation of races (desegregation is the removal of segregation)

separatism in US racial matters, separate development and institutions for whites and African Americans, not excluding the possibility of separate countries

sermon speech on moral or religious matters, usually given in a church

sharecropper tenant farmer who pays part of his crop as rent to the owner of the land

shrine sacred place or building, often where prayers are said for a particular dead person or god

sit-in method of protest, involving sitting down and refusing to be moved

slum area of cheap, overcrowded, inadequate housing inhabitated by poorer people

socialism political system which puts more stress on the needs of the community than on those of the individual

the South in the USA, usually those south-eastern states that made up the Confederate side in the American Civil War. Southerners are people who live there.

Supreme Court the judicial arm of the US government, whose rulings must be observed throughout the USA

unconstitutional in the USA, against the constitution and therefore illegal

Unitarian type of Christian

Untouchables members of the hereditary under-class of Indian society, who do the lowliest, dirtiest jobs

utopian something that would be perfect but is probably impossible to achieve

voter registration campaign to make sure that everyone who can be registered is registered, and is therefore able to vote

whitewashing clearing of blame

Index

Titles in the *Leading Lives* series include:

Hardback   0 431 13865 6

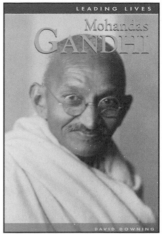

Hardback   0 431 13868 0

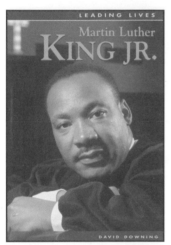

Hardback   0 431 13867 2

Hardback   0 431 13864 8

Hardback   0 431 13869 9

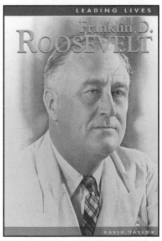

Hardback   0 431 13852 4

Find out about the other titles in this series on our website www.heinemann.co.uk/library